A Stoic's Guide to the 21st Century
Living Virtuously in the Modern World

Table of Contents

1. Introduction ... 1
2. Understanding Stoicism: A Historical Overview ... 2
    - 2.1. The Birth of Stoicism ... 2
    - 2.2. The Early Stoics ... 2
    - 2.3. The Roman Stoics ... 3
    - 2.4. Stoic Principles ... 3
    - 2.5. Stoicism's Relevance Today ... 4
3. The Core Concepts of Stoicism in the Modern Context ... 6
    - 3.1. Understanding the Dichotomy of Control ... 6
    - 3.2. The Stoic Virtues ... 7
    - 3.3. The Concept of Indifferents ... 8
    - 3.4. Practicing Stoic Mindfulness (Prosoche) ... 8
    - 3.5. The View of Passion and Emotion ... 9
4. Practical Stoicism: Rethinking Control and Freedom ... 10
    - 4.1. Understanding the Dichotomy of Control ... 10
    - 4.2. Embracing the Freedom of Indifference ... 11
    - 4.3. Flexing Your Circle of Influence ... 11
    - 4.4. Cultivating Inner Freedom ... 12
    - 4.5. Harnessing Freedom to Act Virtuously ... 12
5. Digital Era Distractions: Lessons from Marcus Aurelius ... 14
    - 5.1. A Glimpse into the Life of Marcus Aurelius ... 14
    - 5.2. The Stoic Perspective on Distractions ... 14
    - 5.3. Wisdom in Aurelius's Word against Digital Distractions ... 15
    - 5.4. Practical Steps against Digital Distractions ... 15
    - 5.5. Living Mindfully in a Digital World ... 16
6. Stoic Virtues: Temperance, Courage, Wisdom, and Justice ... 18
    - 6.1. Temperance ... 18
    - 6.2. Courage ... 19

- 6.3. Wisdom ... 19
- 6.4. Justice ... 20
- 7. Embracing Stoic Mindset for Personal Development ... 21
  - 7.1. Understanding Stoicism ... 21
  - 7.2. Imbibing Stoic Virtues ... 22
  - 7.3. Adopting a Stoic View on Need and Wealth ... 22
  - 7.4. Cultivating Resilience and Equanimity ... 23
  - 7.5. Reshaping Relationships with a Stoic Lens ... 23
  - 7.6. Embracing Failure ... 24
- 8. Mental Resilience: Stoicism and Coping with Stress ... 25
  - 8.1. Shaping the Stoic Mindset ... 25
  - 8.2. Emphasizing Virtue and Benevolence ... 26
  - 8.3. Fostering Amor Fati: Love of Fate ... 26
  - 8.4. Visualizing Negative Events: Premeditatio Malorum ... 27
  - 8.5. Cultivating Mental Tranquility ... 27
  - 8.6. Strategies for Resilience in Daily Life ... 28
- 9. Living Mindfully: The Stoic Perspective on Conscious Living ... 29
  - 9.1. Engaging with the Imperative of Mindfulness ... 29
  - 9.2. From Distraction to Akrateia ... 30
  - 9.3. Stoic Meditation: Prosoche ... 30
  - 9.4. Everyday Mindfulness: The View from Above ... 31
  - 9.5. Stoicism and Modern Mindfulness: Meeting Points ... 31
- 10. Relationships and Community: Applying Stoicism in Social Relations ... 33
  - 10.1. Stoic Principles and Social Relations ... 33
  - 10.2. Seeking Understanding through Stoic Wisdom ... 34
  - 10.3. Empathy and Acceptance: Foundations of Stoic Relations ... 34
  - 10.4. The Role of Integrity and Sincerity ... 35
  - 10.5. Conflict Management through Stoicism ... 35
  - 10.6. Building Communities with Stoic Principles ... 36

11. Moving Forward with Stoicism: A Lifelong Journey of Self-Improvement ... 37
    11.1. Stoicism: A Timeless Approach ... 37
    11.2. The Four Cardinal Virtues ... 37
    11.3. Embracing the Dichotomy of Control ... 38
    11.4. Acceptance and Amor Fati ... 38
    11.5. Using Negative Visualization ... 38
    11.6. Practicing Mindfulness and The View from Above ... 39
    11.7. Stoicism and Relationships ... 39
    11.8. Overcoming Obstacles with Stoic Resilience ... 39
    11.9. Consistent Practice for Lifelong Journey ... 39

Chapter 1. Introduction

Welcome to a remarkable journey that marries the wisdom of the ancients with contemporary life! Our Special Report, "A Stoic's Guide to the 21st Century: Living Virtuously in the Modern World" is an exceptionally engaging exploration that bridges the gap between the time-tested philosophy of stoicism and the unprecedented challenges of today's world. Weaving together thoughtful analyses, expert insights, and practical steps, any reader, whether a novice or an expert, can garner profound insights to enrich their lives. This isn't your typical philosophy manuscipt, it's a life-altering manual tailored for the 21st century! Immerse yourself in this narrative, strengthen the virtues that life demands, and learn to embrace every circumstance with equanimity. Is there a better investment than in a guide to serene, fulfilled living? Read today, thrive tomorrow!

Chapter 2. Understanding Stoicism: A Historical Overview

Stoicism, a philosophical lens that has shaped civilizations across centuries, can be intimidating at first. It might seem nested in niche terms and ancient texts, but its core teachings remain relevant to the modern world —a beacon guiding us towards wisdom, serenity, and virtuous living. This journey back in time seeks to demystify the seemingly complex tenets of Stoicism, providing a platform for our readers to delve deeper into its applications in the 21st Century.

2.1. The Birth of Stoicism

Stoicism was conceived around 300 BCE by Zeno of Citium, a merchant who turned to philosophy following a shipwreck that wiped out his wealth. The teachings of Zeno, neatly encapsulating the essence of comfort found in adversity, found a home in the Stoa Poikile, or Painted Porch, a public space in Athens — attributing their name 'Stoicism'.

Zeno's philosophical leanings were influenced by the teachings of Socrates and the Cynics, but he brought forth a novel perspective, positing that one could only achieve happiness (eudaimonia) through accepting fate and living in accordance with nature and the universe's rational order (logos).

2.2. The Early Stoics

After Zeno, came a line of Stoic heads in the Painted Porch — notably Cleanthes and Chrysippus. Cleanthes, originally a boxer, is known for his perseverance and dedication, often seen working menial jobs during the day and studying philosophy at night. His most significant contribution is the 'Hymn to Zeus', effectively outlining the Stoic worldview.

Chrysippus, considered the second founder of Stoicism, gave structure and academic rigor to these teachings. His work on logic, especially on implication and propositional logic, laid the groundwork for future Stoic philosophers.

2.3. The Roman Stoics

Emerging from its Greek roots, Stoicism found fertile ground in Rome by the late Republic era. Stoic philosophers played pivotal roles in Roman society, teaching emperors, advising statesmen, and authoring texts that shape our understanding of Stoicism today.

Most notably:

- Seneca - Nero's tutor and advisor, and a driven statesman, Seneca's writings provide a rich understanding of Stoicism, addressing themes like anger management, the shortness of life, and the practice of philosophy.
- Epictetus - An ex-slave who rose to become prominent philosopher, Epictetus offered discourses and 'The Enchiridion', focusing heavily on Stoic ethics and the concept of controlling inner emotional responses to external events.
- Marcus Aurelius - The Roman Emperor wrote 'Meditations', a series of personal notebooks, contemplations offering profound insights into Stoic philosophy, all the while running an empire in tumultuous times.

2.4. Stoic Principles

Stoicism predicates on a few key principles:

1. Logos: Acknowledging that the universe follows a rational and divine order, and aligning one's life to it.
2. Virtue: Advocating a virtuous life, steeped in wisdom, courage, justice, and temperance - the ultimate good.
3. Dichotomy of control: Accepting that while certain things are under our control (actions, thoughts), others are not (external events).
4. Emotional detachment: Maintaining equanimity by distancing oneself from misguided emotions and acknowledging the transient nature of human life.

2.5. Stoicism's Relevance Today

As much as Stoicism is rooted in antiquity, its teachings remain a guiding force in today's world, offering ways to navigate modern complexities. By allowing us to recognise our ability to control our responses and emotions, it delivers emotional resilience in an uncertain world.

The wisdom of the ancients remains relevant, continuing to inspire philosophers and thinkers. Stoicism, with its focus on internal strength and resilience, offers an avenue to peace and fulfillment in the chaotic modern landscape, a testament to the enduring power of this philosophical school.

Like much of philosophy, Stoicism isn't a one-size-fits-all doctrine, but it offers the opportunity to build a mental model for Stoic living. In the subsequent chapter, we delve into these principles and show how we could apply them to our lives. As we journey into the 21st Century, let's journey together to understand and learn from this ancient philosophy that continues to resonate and offer profound insight into the human condition.

Stoicism is more than a school of thought or a philosophy; it's a lens through which we can view the world and our place in it - a lens that, despite millennia, continues to offer clarity to those who seek it. As such, understanding its origins and tenets is the first step in appreciating its teachings and ability to shape a virtuous life amidst modernity's myriad challenges.

Chapter 3. The Core Concepts of Stoicism in the Modern Context

The compelling potency of Stoicism lies in its premises, which have surprisingly pertinent relevance to the peculiar demands of the 21st century. There exists a prevalent misconception asserting that Stoicism requires turning oneself into an impassive automaton. This couldn't be farther from the truth. In fact, Stoicism is a philosophy developed by thoughtful individuals aimed at maximizing potential happiness by placing control exactly where it belongs, within oneself. It does so by emphasizing the distinction between what we can change and what we cannot.

3.1. Understanding the Dichotomy of Control

A crucial starting point in Stoicism is recognizing the `Dichotomy of Control`, an idea clarified by the Roman Stoic philosopher Epictetus. This principle asserts that some things are within our control and others are not. The things within our control are our own actions, thoughts, and reactions, whereas the things beyond our control include external events, such as natural disasters, other people's actions, or the passing of time.

In the context of our fast-paced, 21st-century lives, this dichotomy remains extremely pertinent. It offers solace and empowerment. For instance, in an age of social media, it is typically effortless to fall into the trap of comparison, leading to dissatisfaction or anger. However, if you apply the Dichotomy of Control, you realize that others' behaviors, lifestyles, or showcased wealth are beyond your control. What is within your command is your reaction: the decision to not let it affect you negatively. By identifying and accepting what you can and cannot control, you are empowered to focus your energy on changing the things you actually can.

3.2. The Stoic Virtues

At the heart of the Stoic philosophy are the Four Cardinal Virtues—Wisdom, Courage, Justice, and Temperance. Though their roots are ancient, they still sit just as comfortably within the framework of modern ethics.

Wisdom, the master virtue, is the knowledge of what is good, what is bad, and what is indifferent. In the modern world, wisdom can be seen as the ability to make good decisions amidst misinformation, to remain calm under pressure, and to think critically in an era where opinions may be swayed by superficial or false information.

Courage, in Stoic thought, isn't simply physical bravery. It embodies moral courage—the courage to do the right thing—even in the face of potential losses, criticism, or dismissal. This form of bravery is particularly pertinent in our society, where standing up for justice and fairness can be fraught with complications and backlash.

Justice refers to the concept of fairness and good interpersonal relationships. If we integrate justice into our lives, we work towards equality, practice empathy, and strive to do good unto others. This has clear implications in our era, when global movements urge us to challenge and eliminate systems of inequality and unfairness.

Temperance, or moderation, is the virtue of self-restraint. This value holds immense importance in an age of consumerism and excess, where delaying gratification and exercising self-control gives us the freedom from being ruled by our desires.

By focusing on cultivating these virtues rather than seeking external validation, Stoics aim for a good and satisfying life. This focus provides a sturdy framework for moral and ethical decisions, also resulting in resilience in the face of adversity.

3.3. The Concept of Indifferents

Stoics further speak of `preferred indifferents` and `dispreferred indifferents`—things that do not affect our moral worth but are naturally preferred or naturally avoided. Wealth, for example, is a preferred indifferent: it is not inherently good or evil, but its use can be.

Recognizing the differentiation of these indifferents is especially crucial in today's world. With the rise of materialism and the tendency to judge success and happiness based on material wealth, remembering the true, indifferent nature of these factors can help maintain our mental equilibrium and satisfaction.

3.4. Practicing Stoic Mindfulness (Prosoche)

`Prosoche`, or Stoic Mindfulness, lies at the heart of Stoic Philosophy. It is the practice of constant self-awareness in order to apply wisdom and the virtues to every thought and action.

In our contemporary world, where distractions are abundant, practicing Prosoche allows one to remain present, focused, and purposeful. It enables conscious, deliberate decisions rather than automatic, reactionary responses. Mental clarity achieved through mindfulness, hence, could be our most powerful tool in navigating the fast-paced, chaotic nature of 21st-century life.

3.5. The View of Passion and Emotion

Contrary to popular belief, Stoics do not advocate for the eradication of emotions—rather, they encourage transforming destructive passions into healthy emotions. They classified pathos (illness of the soul, including destructive passions like fear, anger, and excessive pleasure) and eupatheiai (healthy feelings that result from the correct use of impressions).

Understanding and implementing this view on emotions can be liberating, especially in our society where emotional peaks and valleys are intensified by the 24/7 news cycle and the constant influx of social media. By discerning between healthy and destructive emotions, we can foster mental resilience and inner peace.

Ultimately, Stoicism equips us with practical tools for navigating life, encouraging rational thinking, emotional fortitude, and ethical living. When applied, its core concepts lend themselves robustly to managing the unique pressures of the 21st century, thereby fostering an existence marked by peace, resilience, and virtue.

Chapter 4. Practical Stoicism: Rethinking Control and Freedom

In a chaotic world that continually pushes us off balance, stoicism offers us a solid footing. It equips us to deal with the unpredictabilities of life, empowering us with a mindset that renders us immune to external circumstances. A pivotal aspect of stoicism revolves around control - understanding what aspects of life we can influence and what parts lie beyond our reach. In many ways, recognizing these boundaries is where our freedom truly starts.

4.1. Understanding the Dichotomy of Control

The core principle of stoicism can be summed up in Epictetus' renowned words, "Some things are in our control and others not." The Stoic Dichotomy of Control encourages us to categorize life's events into those we can control—like our actions, judgments, desires, and aversions—and those we cannot—like other people's actions or attitudes, the weather, or the past. This understanding becomes the bedrock of stoic tranquility.

However, understanding this dichotomy isn't enough; we must also internalize it. For example, you cannot control the weather, so it is irrational to be upset by it. In contrast, you do have control over how you prepare for and react to it. Our emotional investment should align with elements that are within our control.

4.2. Embracing the Freedom of Indifference

The Stoics believed that freedom in the truest sense comes from indifference to things beyond our control. They termed this 'apatheia,' which means a state of mind where one isn't disturbed by the passions. Although this sounds nuanced, it does not promote emotional disconnect; instead, it encourages emotional wisdom where the unnecessary, irrational, and harmful passions are kept at bay.

Let's consider a universal scenario - dealing with a traffic jam. You may feel anger bubbling up as the car honks pierce the air. But if you apply the Stoic principle, you understand the traffic and it's resulting delay (an external event) is out of your control. What you do have control over is your response. In this case, perhaps you could capitalize on the unexpected free time by listening to an audiobook or practicing mindful breathing. This reframed attitude stems from a state of indifference towards the external event, letting you seize control of your internal state.

4.3. Flexing Your Circle of Influence

One might question, do Stoics passively accept everything that occurs? The answer is no. Stoicism isn't about fatalistic surrender. The Stoics do advise us to concern ourselves primarily with the things under our control, but that does not mean ignoring everything else. Rather, Stoics invite us to categorize the uncontrollables into those that we hold no influence over (like the past, or the laws of nature) and those where our actions might not guarantee an outcome, but can certainly affect the situation.

Such a distinction helps define our 'Circle of Influence'. Even in the traffic jam scenario, you could decide to leave earlier next time or pick a different route. As the Stoic philosopher Marcus Aurelius puts it, "You have power over your mind - not outside events. Realize this, and you will find strength".

4.4. Cultivating Inner Freedom

Stoicism shines a light on the path to genuine freedom, which dwells within our thoughts, perceptions, and actions. Your inner mental state, your voluntary actions, and direct judgments—these are your dominion. When we fully grasp this, we experience a sense of freedom that physical bonds or external circumstances cannot quell.

How, then, do we cultivate this state of inner freedom? Through the relentless practice of awareness and reflection. We train ourselves to pause, to observe our reactions to events around us, and to ask ourselves, "Is this under my control?" If the answer is no, we strive to accept it and move towards liberation from unnecessary distress. If yes, we contemplate the best action steps and invest our energy judiciously.

4.5. Harnessing Freedom to Act Virtuously

Indeed, the Stoic concept of freedom isn't a pursuit for libertine behavior. Instead, it's about creating space for virtuous actions. The end goal is to be unperturbed by things outside our control, allowing for focused energy in areas where we can exert positive influence.

Remember, for Stoics, virtue is the only good. Therefore, an essential part of the freedom-control dynamic is ensuring our freedom leads to virtue—an upright character and honorable actions. When we get upset about a political issue, for instance, we don't just accept the status quo because it's out of our immediate control. We channel our energy into meaningful action. That might mean educating ourselves or others on the matter, campaigning for our cause, or voting accordingly.

In this modern world, this ancient wisdom brings to light a control-freedom paradigm that empowers us to live more harmonious, fulfilled lives. By discerning the elements within our control and acting virtuously with resolute indifference to external events, we carve out an internal fortress of tranquility and freedom, imperturbable amidst life's storm. This is the heart of practical Stoicism: a handbook for serene, empowering living, irrespective of external circumstances. Translate understanding into action, and free yourself from the confines of external control. You are, after all, the architect of your inner peace.

Chapter 5. Digital Era Distractions: Lessons from Marcus Aurelius

Today, in the age of smartphone addiction and endless social media scrolling, it seems impossible to find a moment's peace. Amid the digital cacophony, the wisdom of ancient Stoic philosopher Marcus Aurelius offers a potent antidote.

5.1. A Glimpse into the Life of Marcus Aurelius

Marcus Aurelius, known as the last of the Five Good Emperors of the Roman Empire, was a model Stoic. Despite his imperial duties and recurrent personal adversities, including wars, plagues, and treacherous political affairs, he remained devoted to stoicism throughout his life. His 'Meditations', a collection of personal writings, lay bare the emperor's inmost thoughts and philosophical exercises and have shaped lives for centuries. They offer a window to navigate the tumultuous waters of the 21st century as well.

5.2. The Stoic Perspective on Distractions

To better understand the Stoic responses to distractions, it is vital to familiarize ourselves with some fundamentals of the Stoic philosophy. Stoicism teaches us that certain things are within our control — our opinions, impulses, desires, aversions, and, in a word, everything of our actions. In contrast, things outside our control include the body, property, reputation, command, and, in one word, everything not of our actions.

From this perspective, the presence of distractions and their potential to draw our attention are not within our control, but how we respond to these distractions, indeed, is. It is important not to yield, but to acknowledge their presence and consciously decide not to engage.

5.3. Wisdom in Aurelius's Word against Digital Distractions

Though digital distractions did not exist in Aurelius's time, the wisdom in his words can certainly be applied to battle them.

+ In Book II, he wrote, "Do not act as if you had ten thousand years to live... while you're alive, while it's in your power, be good." It urges us to value our time as our most precious resource, which is not to be wasted in distraction, but used effectively.

+ He also advised, "Always make a definition or sketch of what presents itself to your mind, so you can see it stripped bare to its essential nature and identify it clearly, in whole and in all its parts". This call for introspection and understanding can be used to assess the nature of digital distractions and how they impact us.

5.4. Practical Steps against Digital Distractions

Despite the overpowering allure of digital devices, here are some practical steps inspired by Marcus Aurelius's teachings that could prove useful:

1. Prioritize: Allocate a specific time for smartphone use or social media. Engaging mindlessly in these activities often comes at the expense of a more valuable use of time.

2. Reflect: Understand what draws you to these platforms repeatedly. Often they are designed to fulfill inner cravings for validation, entertainment, or a sense of belonging.

3. Take Control: Marcus Aurelius stressed on the control we can exert on our thoughts and actions. Instead of being controlled by digital literature, aim to use them as tools serving your purposes.

4. Be Mindful: Consider each moment spent distracted as a moment lost. Strive to make the most of every moment.

5.5. Living Mindfully in a Digital World

Although distractions abound in the digital era, it doesn't mean we have to succumb to them. Marcus Aurelius encouraged the cultivation of an inner fortress, a place of refuge from external disturbances. This fortress is built from virtues such as wisdom, justice, courage, and self-control.

Using Stoic teachings, we can learn to foster a capacity for self-awareness that helps us distinguish between what's within our control and what isn't. With persistent practice, we can learn to maintain equanimity in the face of the endlessly stimulating digital world.

The purpose isn't to totally shun technology or digital devices, but to utilize them judiciously. At its core, a stoic is indifferent to the means; it is the ends that matter — leading a fulfilled, virtuous life. Therefore, these devices could very well be tools aiding us on our stoic journey, so long as they are used mindfully and wisely, and not as inescapable masters of our time and attention.

In the end, living virtuously in the digital world is not about resisting its conveniences, but mastering internal responses to external stimuli, choosing attentiveness over distraction, and serenity over restlessness. With Marcus Aurelius as our guide, we can reclaim our digital lives, rebuild our attention spans, and find serenity amid the clamor.

Chapter 6. Stoic Virtues: Temperance, Courage, Wisdom, and Justice

The stoic philosophy established four cardinal virtues as the cornerstones of righteous living: temperance, courage, wisdom, and justice. Derived from the beliefs of some of the most enlightened minds in ancient Greece, these virtues offer a compelling code of personal ethics that remain highly relevant in our modern world. By understanding and applying these virtues, we can navigate the labyrinth of life with composure and moral integrity.

6.1. Temperance

Temperance, known in Greek as sophrosyne, is defined as a sort of disciplined moderation or self-control. It is about controlling one's impulses and desires, learning not to indulge in excess, and maintaining a balanced sense in everything we do. It's the capacity to resist temptation and not to give into immediate gratifications, but instead foster prudent choices that benefit us in the long run.

Living in a time of unprecedented access and convenience, we are constantly exposed to allurements that encourage indulgence, be it food, entertainment, or technology. Following the stoic virtue of temperance, however, we learn to manage these attractions pragmatically without being caged by them.

Practical application of temperance could include mindful eating, screen time management, or even setting personal boundaries in relationships. It is a call to sift out our wants from our needs, and to fortify ourselves against the storm of sensory overstimulation that often characterizes modern life.

6.2. Courage

Courage or andreia in Greek, is not just about physical bravery, but also the mental fortitude to face uncertainties, adversities, and fear. It's about standing firm on our principles, unswayed by external influences, and taking appropriate actions even when they are risky or demanding.

In terms of 21st-century living, courage is vital for us to move beyond our comfort zone. It is needed when we must embrace change, confront injustices, or make tough decisions. At a time when many of us suffer from a fear of failure or rejection, learning to foster courage can provide a lifeline to successfully traverse life's difficult terrains.

To practically nurture courage, we could challenge ourselves with new tasks, speak our minds when it's necessary, assume accountability for our actions, and, fundamentally, learn to accept failure as a stepping stone towards personal growth.

6.3. Wisdom

Wisdom or phronesis is the ability to discern or judge what is true, right, or lasting. It is the capacity to make sound judgments and decisions based on personal knowledge and experience. Fostering wisdom invites rational thinking, clarity of thought, and an open mind to learn from every experience - good or bad.

In our data-driven era, bombarded with torrents of information, wisdom helps us sift truth from falsehood and make informed decisions. It encourages us to be lifelong learners, mentally agile, and open to different perspectives. Wisdom is deeply ingrained in self-awareness, emotional intelligence, and observation, all key skills for surviving and thriving in our complex world.

To cultivate wisdom, we should seek out diverse experiences and perspectives, remain curious and constantly adaptable, and practice mindfulness to stay connected with our inner selves and the external world.

6.4. Justice

Justice or dikaiosyne implies fairness, righteousness, and balance. It's the virtue that guides us to act with equity and fairness towards others, acknowledging and respecting their rights and dignity.

In today's interconnected world, justice magnifies our responsibility as global citizens. It informs us about our role in the socio-economic and political landscapes not only within our immediate communities but also globally. As disparities and biases continue to challenge societies, it's our sense of justice that encourages us to act for equality and rightfulness.

To apply justice in everyday life, we can promote fairness and resist discriminatory behavior in our respective spheres, engage in activism or governance to bring about social change, and contribute to causes that alleviate inequality and suffering.

To conclude, these four stoic virtues: temperance, courage, wisdom, and justice, grant us a clear road map to live purposefully and ethically in the 21st century. They provide a strong moral compass, fostering resilience and inner peace amidst the ceaseless ebbs and flows of modern life. The nurturing of these virtues is a continuous journey, acting as a beacon to guide us towards fulfillment and contentment, irrespective of external circumstances.

Chapter 7. Embracing Stoic Mindset for Personal Development

Beginning your journey of personal development requires understanding the unmatched strength and resilience of the human spirit—a gift that has been bestowed upon every individual. Stoicism, with its pillars of wisdom, courage, justice, and temperance, offers a powerful blueprint to unlock this inherent potential. By embracing a Stoic mindset, you not only prepare to weather the storms of life but also enhance the quality of your personal and professional relationships.

7.1. Understanding Stoicism

Stoicism, a philosophical school that dates back to ancient Greece, focuses on fostering virtues like wisdom, self-control, and courage to achieve tranquility and fulfilment. This philosophy thrives on the notion that while we cannot control external events, we do have absolute control over our beliefs, perspectives, and reactions.

The cornerstone of Stoicism is its emphasis on our power to mold our impressions. For instance, consider a situation where you receive harsh criticism. While our usual response might be dejection or anger, Stoicism teaches us that the criticism itself does not inflict pain. Rather, it's our interpretation of the situation that determines our response. Through a Stoic lens, one can see such criticism as not a personal attack, but a chance to grow, learn, and improve.

Remember, a Stoic's journey is not about curbing emotions. Rather, it is about understanding them, letting the negative ones flow out and using the positive ones to enhance our acceptance of what life offers.

7.2. Imbibing Stoic Virtues

First, let's delve deeper into the four main Stoic virtues: Wisdom, Courage, Justice, and Temperance.

1. **Wisdom**: Wisdom is about making rational and morally sound decisions. It is the correct judgment necessary for the resolution of various life predicaments. Stoicism advocates wisdom as a trait than can move mountains, clear foggy paths, and guide individuals to lead a virtuous life.
2. **Courage**: Stoic courage is not merely about physical bravery but also about having the mental fortitude to confront difficulties, persevere through challenges, and move forward despite failures or adverse conditions.
3. **Justice**: Justice here is not only about observing the law, but understanding and acting according to the very foundation of fairness and goodwill in human interactions. It's about being respectful and showing kindness and understanding.
4. **Temperance**: This virtue refers to self-restraint and moderation, be it in emotions or indulgences. Temperance helps to avoid extremes and maintains balance in all facets of life.

Embedding these virtues in our character requires consistent practice. By consciously aligning our thoughts and actions with these virtues, we program ourselves to act virtuously out of habit, rather than only in times of conscious effort.

7.3. Adopting a Stoic View on Need and Wealth

Epictetus, one of the most significant Stoic philosophers, elucidated that being rich is not about owning the most, but needing the least. Stoics emphasise taking life down to the basics, diminishing our wants, and appreciating the simple and unadulterated pleasures of life.

In the 21st Century, consumerism can create a never-ending cycle of insatiability. Hence, a Stoic mindset becomes all the more crucial. Moving beyond materialistic desire and developing contentment with what we have plays a significant role in leading a fulfilled life.

7.4. Cultivating Resilience and Equanimity

Resilience, the capacity to recover from difficulties and maintain mental fortitude, is a central tenet of Stoicism. Stoics discover how to choose their reactions wisely, aligning them with nature's laws, and, in the process, forge an unshakeable resilience.

Meanwhile, equanimity, or maintaining a calm and composed state in all situations, supports resilience. It allows us to remain steady in moments of success and failure, pleasure and pain, thereby freeing us from the highs and lows of extreme emotions.

To cultivate resilience and equanimity, practice mindfulness. Mindfulness encourages us to understand our thoughts and feelings without judgement. This non-reactive awareness increases our capacity to endure hardships while maintaining inner tranquility.

7.5. Reshaping Relationships with a Stoic Lens

Stoicism can immensely improve how we interact with others. Stoics advocate treating every person with respect and understanding, as each individual holds innate dignity and value.

Stoic philosophy promotes the idea of seeing each person as a fellow member of the human community. By adopting a Stoic mindset, we can transform how we perceive and deal with others, leading to more compassionate, understanding, and harmonious relationships.

7.6. Embracing Failure

The fear of failing often holds people back from pursuing new opportunities or exploring their potential. However, in Stoicism, failure is a blessing disguised as a teacher. By reframing the concept of failure as simply the occurrence of a reality different than expected, one can use these experiences to learn, grow, and develop resilience.

Stoics view hardships as challenges, rather than obstacles. This perspective delivers a sense of power and autonomy over personal development.

In conclusion, embracing a Stoic mindset for personal development involves embodying cardinal virtues, adopting mindful awareness, reshaping our perspective on needs and wealth, and viewing hardships as opportunities for learning. By integrating these teachings into daily life, we can cultivate the ability to handle any situation with grace, enhance our relationships, and lead a fulfilling life.

Chapter 8. Mental Resilience: Stoicism and Coping with Stress

In the realms of adversity, chaos, and tumultuous events, the cultivation of mental resilience becomes paramount. Harnessing the wisdom of stoic philosophy, we are equipped to withstand and even flourish amidst life's trials. The eminent Marcus Aurelius wrote, "You have power over your mind - not outside events. Realize this, and you will find strength." With this mindset, the concepts contained within this chapter will arm you with everything you need to nurture your resilience and cope with stress most efficiently.

8.1. Shaping the Stoic Mindset

Ingenuous as it might seem, the first step toward resilience is defining and understanding the true stoic mindset. It isn't about seclusion or emotion suppression, but rather about acceptance and contextualization. A stoic focuses on accepting circumstances beyond control and placing emphasis on personal response over external events. Stoic philosopher Epictetus astutely said, "It's not what happens to you, but how you react to it that matters." Expanding upon this tenet, mental resilience is not just about weathering hardships but also how those hardships are processed and handled. It is this conscious choice of reaction, in essence, that shapes the stoic mindset.

To practice this, begin by separating events into what is within your control and what isn't. By worrying less about uncontrollable circumstances and concentrating on your actions, decisions, and emotions, you direct your energy where it can genuinely make a difference.

8.2. Emphasizing Virtue and Benevolence

A core pillar of stoicism involves honing virtue and ensuring this guides your life. It is virtue that redirects our behavior toward the noble and good, a beacon through life's storms. High-stress situations can sometimes blur our moral compass, but a stoic remains anchored to virtue amidst the chaos.

The Stoics considered four core virtues: wisdom, courage, justice, and temperance. Consider these virtues as your moral compass when dealing with stress or adversity. They inform your decisions, your reactions, and your general demeanor. To the Stoics, these virtues were more than rules; they were a lifestyle. Cultivating these virtues fosters an inner strength that continually prepares you for life's curveballs.

8.3. Fostering Amor Fati: Love of Fate

Sometimes, life's winds blow us further off-course than we could ever have imagined. However, the practice of "amor fati," or a love of fate, teaches us to embrace those winds as a natural part of life, even part of its beauty. Nietzsche described it perfectly, "Not merely bear what is necessary, still less conceal it... but love it."

How does one start fostering amor fati in the face of looming stress? Techniques to develop this include mindfulness - being aware of the present moment - and radical acceptance - welcoming life as it comes. It also means finding opportunities in adversity, seeing every setback as a chance for growth, learning, and new possibilities.

8.4. Visualizing Negative Events: Premeditatio Malorum

Stoics advocate a practice known as premeditatio malorum, literally translating to "the premeditation of evils." This may sound negative, but the goal is quite the opposite. It involves the mental rehearsal of potential adversities or unwelcome events. The idea is to imagine things going wrong, not to elicit fear, but to reduce the psychological impact if the event does occur.

Thinking clearly when under huge stress is tough, and practicing premeditatio malorum allows us to put our theoretical principles into action in a controlled emotional environment. It is, in essence, a stress rehearsal that allows you to cultivate resilience before the tumult hits.

8.5. Cultivating Mental Tranquility

Achieving a calm, tranquil mind in the face of hardship is a skill like any other; it requires practice. Seneca speaks of tranquillity as the ultimate consequence of a well-led life, which includes accepting one's fate and concentrating on virtue. The tranquillity of mind doesn't represent a lack of emotion but a state where the mind remains unflustered by external events.

To cultivate tranquillity, meditate and practice regular mindfulness, focusing on the present. Also, practice visualizing calmness in stressful scenarios, maintaining perspective, and using stoic principles to cultivate tranquillity.

8.6. Strategies for Resilience in Daily Life

Implementing these stoic principles and practices into daily life might seem like an uphill task. But, rest assured, incorporating this profound wisdom into your routine can be less daunting than it sounds.

- Start by maintaining a journal. Write down daily experiences, thoughts, and emotions. Reflect on where you have control and where you don't.
- Make deliberate choices based on your defined virtues. Let these guide your actions and reactions.
- Practice mindfulness and meditation daily. Use this time to dig deep into self-understanding and awareness.
- Regularly visualize yourself navigating stressful situations calmly.
- Learn to see setbacks and failures as opportunities to grow and learn.

By nurturing a stoic philosophy and incorporating it into your daily life, you will build mental resilience that is immune to the chaos of external circumstances. Stress will be a part of life, but with resilience, it doesn't have to rule your life. As Seneca elegantly puts it, "A gem cannot be polished without friction, nor a man perfected without trials." We must embrace what we cannot change, focus on what we can, and hitch our minds to the perennial wisdom of the Stoics to lead a fulfilled life.

Chapter 9. Living Mindfully: The Stoic Perspective on Conscious Living

With hyper-connectivity, incessant notifications, and ever-mounting to-do lists, the modern world swirls around in a vortex of relentless activity. Against this backdrop, the ancient practice of Stoicism remains ever relevant.

Living mindfully, as suggested by Stoicism, is really about paying attention; it's about being aware of our own thoughts and actions, as well as the world around us. It's about taming the wandering mind and joining it with the body in the present moment.

9.1. Engaging with the Imperative of Mindfulness

Mindfulness, in Stoic philosophy, is first a virtue and then a practice. It is a form of clear, non-judgmental, and wholehearted attentiveness to what is happening in the present. From a Stoic perspective, to live mindfully is to live virtuously. Contrary to its misgivings, being in the 'here and now' doesn't demand ascetic renunciation of worldly commitments. Instead, it champions the radical idea of connecting more fully, consciously, and authentically with the world.

Marcus Aurelius, the Stoic king-emperor, underlined this when he said, "A man's true delight is to do the things he was made for". To act mindfully is to engage with the tasks of the moment with a sense of purpose and care, whether it's a high-stake business meeting or washing the dishes at home.

9.2. From Distraction to Akrateia

One of the enemies of mindfulness is distraction. A distracted mind is not grounded in the present. It's always somewhere else. This restlessness is not just a cause of mental discomfort, but also a potential moral failing. If we are not present, we cannot make informed, rational decisions; we may act impulsively, and not in line with our highest values.

The Stoics had a term for this: 'akrateia', or the lack of self-control. Akrateia is a condition where we cannot align our actions with our knowledge of what's good for us. We might know that checking our smartphones every five minutes doesn't add value to our lives, yet we do it nonetheless.

To overcome akrateia, Stoicism suggests a mindful course correction that checks the power of the 'impressions' upon us. These impressions can be anything our senses perceive or thoughts we are having. Every time an impression arises, we have the power to accept, reject, or remain indifferent to it.

9.3. Stoic Meditation: Prosoche

Stoics practiced a form of meditation known as 'prosoche', or 'mindful attention'. Different from eastern meditations that observe breath or bodily sensations, prosoche rests on a rational, self-aware mindset. It involves being attentive to our impressions, judgments, and reactions, and reflecting on them with a sense of detachment.

You may leverage prosoche in two steps. First, pause as impressions arise, and evaluate them as unbiasedly as possible. Then, once the impression is acknowledged and dissected, intentionally decide whether to discard it or engage with it. This process helps develop equanimity and reduces irrational emotional responses to external events.

9.4. Everyday Mindfulness: The View from Above

Aside from the daily practice of prosoche, Stoics recommend another exercise: the 'View from Above'. This practice starts with focusing on your immediate surroundings and then conceptually expanding the focus to encompass your local community, your city, the country, the Earth, the solar system, all the way up to our infinite universe. This exercise is designed to contextualize our problems and worries, helping us achieve a balanced perspective.

In modern times, when anxiety, stress, and relentless forward-focused ambitions may overwhelm us, such a view taps into a broader vista of time and space.

9.5. Stoicism and Modern Mindfulness: Meeting Points

While Stoicism originated over two millennia ago and modern mindfulness stems largely from 20th-century reinterpretations of Buddhist practices, there are noteworthy convergences. Both encourage attention and awareness, both underline impermanence, and both promote a non-judgmental response to experiences.

Learning to engage with life mindfully, the Stoic way, embodies a key pillar of the philosophy. When we stop sleepwalking through our lives, and instead, experience it with purposeful attentiveness, we become the rational, virtuous beings the stoics intended us to be.

Nourishing the virtue of mindfulness armed with Stoic insights is not just about personal growth. It is also about equipping ourselves to contribute meaningfully to the broader human story unfolding around us. The Stoic call to mindfulness is a call to awaken—to our potential, to the wisdom within us, and to the world we exist in. From living more to living better, Stoic mindfulness is your guiding star. It reminds you that you can indeed navigate the frenetic pace of the 21st century by anchoring yourself in the moment.

Chapter 10. Relationships and Community: Applying Stoicism in Social Relations

Stoicism, a philosophy that emerged in the Hellenistic period, holds timeless insights about dealing with life's situations, and is especially pertinent in our interactions within relationships and communities. It offers a tranquility and peace of mind that arises from understanding and accepting the world as it is. This chapter provides practical guidance on applying Stoic principles to social relations. We will explore how to establish meaningful relationships, build stronger communities, and manage conflict using Stoicism's wisdom.

10.1. Stoic Principles and Social Relations

Stoic philosophers, including Epictetus, Marcus Aurelius, and Seneca, emphasized that our relationships are of paramount importance, along with our virtue of character. We are inherently social beings, and hence, our interactions form a crucial part of our existence. Stoicism posits that these interactions should be rooted in wisdom and kindness, paving the way for harmonious social relations.

From Stoic philosophy, we can derive three fundamental principles to apply in our relationships:

- Seek to understand before being understood.
- Practice empathy and acceptance.
- Act with integrity and sincerity.

These principles form the foundation of Stoic social relations, guiding us on how to navigate the complex web that constitutes our personal and professional relationships.

10.2. Seeking Understanding through Stoic Wisdom

The first principle prompts us to seek to understand others before expecting to be understood. Stoicism explains that human perception, interpretation, and reactions largely depend on our internal mental models. Epictetus famously said, "We have two ears and one mouth so that we can listen twice as much as we speak." By enhancing our listening skills and seeking to comprehend others' perspectives, we can cultivate harmonious relationships.

Stoic exercises like "the View from Above" can help us in comprehending others' perspectives. This practice encourages us to zoom out and view situations from a third-person perspective, providing a broader outlook and aiding in comprehending others' stance in any given situation.

10.3. Empathy and Acceptance: Foundations of Stoic Relations

Another crucial component in Stoic social relations is empathy and acceptance. Stoicism urges us to empathize with others by recognizing that everyone is facing their own battles, and respond with compassion and kindness. Understanding this lends us the capacity to accept others for who they are, creating deeper and more meaningful relationships.

Furthermore, Stoicism reminds us that we cannot control others' actions or reactions, but we can control our attitudes and responses. This principle of acceptance involves recognizing other people's ability to think and act independently, and we can mitigate misunderstandings and conflict by embracing this reality.

10.4. The Role of Integrity and Sincerity

Integrity and sincerity are core virtues in Stoicism, and they propagate authenticity in our relationships. Stoics believed in living according to nature, which fundamentally means living authentically and ethically, in alignment with our core virtues. When we act with sincerity, we foster trust, one of the pillars of strong relationships.

Marcus Aurelius suggested living each day as though it was our last, meaning, we should communicate sincerely and openly, leaving no room for regret. When we approach relations with sincerity and integrity, we create clarity and trust, enriching our bonds with others.

10.5. Conflict Management through Stoicism

Despite our best efforts, we might occasionally face conflicts in our relationships. Stoicism provides tools for conflict resolution, predicated on the principle of not reacting impulsively to external events. Instead, Stoics urge us to pause and reflect, allowing our own mental and emotional upheaval to settle before responding.

In such a scenario, dichotomy of control comes into play where we ascertain what is within our control (our reactions, emotions) and what is not (other's actions, external events). By focusing only on what we control, we can mitigate conflict effectively and preserve our equanimity.

10.6. Building Communities with Stoic Principles

Applying these Stoic principles at a larger scale, we can build stronger, more connected communities. Remember, our Stoic virtue extends beyond our personal relationships to how we contribute to the society at large.

Using Stoic practices of empathy and acceptance, we can promote inclusivity and acceptance in our community. Such an approach fosters feelings of unity and cohesion, creating a harmonious, prosperous society.

In conclusion, Stoic philosophy provides an incredibly robust framework to navigate our social relations. By internalizing these principles and making them a part of our everyday interactions, we can cultivate meaningful relationships and contribute to building strong communities. Minds steeped in Stoic wisdom improve individual well-being and propagate the same in their relationships, ultimately leading to a more aware and compassionate society.

Chapter 11. Moving Forward with Stoicism: A Lifelong Journey of Self-Improvement

The path of Stoic philosophy is not a one-time encounter but an ongoing journey of self-discovery, personal development, and continual growth. As you take your first step on this path, remind yourself consistently that the journey is the destination. Keeping this in mind, it is brilliant for one to contemplate ways to incorporate Stoic virtues in day-to-day life, gracefully accepting life's turmoil while cherishing its beauty.

11.1. Stoicism: A Timeless Approach

The ancient philosophy of Stoicism, emerging from Greece and Rome, is as relevant today as it was over 2,000 years ago. The Stoic sages like Seneca, Epictetus, and Marcus Aurelius shared wisdom to navigate life's inherent challenges. Their teachings encourage us to gain control over our reactions, work towards emotional resilience, and foster a sense of inner peace. Stoicism's key foundation lies in understanding factors within our control and those beyond it, imbuing our actions with wisdom, courage, justice, and temperance.

11.2. The Four Cardinal Virtues

To follow the path of Stoicism fully, it's pivotal to comprehend and embody the Four Cardinal Virtices: wisdom, courage, justice, and temperance. Wisdom empowers us to think clearly, make decisions rationally and see the world as it is. Courage emboldens us to face challenges, bear hardships and confront our weaknesses. Justice instills an unwavering dedication to fairness, honesty, and integrity. Temperance, meanwhile, guides us to exercise self-restraint, practice moderation, and avoid excesses.

11.3. Embracing the Dichotomy of Control

A significant axiom of Stoic philosophy is the dichotomy of control. It underscores the understanding that some events are within our control — our opinions, motivations, desires, and, above all, our responses to external circumstances. Meanwhile, many factors in life lie beyond our control: the actions of others, the natural world, and the past or future. The dichotomy of control teaches us to focus our energy on what we can influence, letting go of what we cannot. This approach leads to a serene and fulfilling existence.

11.4. Acceptance and Amor Fati

Amor Fati, a Latin phrase, translates to "love of fate." This concept is at the heart of Stoicism. It encourages embracing all aspects of life — the good, the bad, and even the seemingly mundane. Amor Fati is not about resignation or passivity; it is a vigorous acceptance of reality. By adopting this, we stop resisting the natural flow of life, thereby experiencing a profound sense of inner peace.

11.5. Using Negative Visualization

Negative visualization is another worthwhile Stoic practice. It involves contemplating the impermanence of life's pleasures, relationships, achievements, even life itself. This practice helps us appreciate what we have, combatting complacency, and preventing hedonic adaptation. It also prepares us for potential adversities, making us resilient in the face of difficulties.

11.6. Practicing Mindfulness and The View from Above

Practicing mindfulness, being fully present in the moment, is also integral to Stoicism. It asks us to be engaged in our current activities fully, fostering gratitude, focus, and equanimity. Similarly, the View from Above technique guides us to visualize ourselves from a higher vantage point, cultivating a broader perspective towards life and its trifling incidents.

11.7. Stoicism and Relationships

Stoicism offers us the tools to develop healthy and fulfilling relationships. By exercising self-restraint and understanding, we learn to respect others' viewpoints and maintain harmony. Additionally, Stoic principles of fairness and kindness advocate for empathetic and supportive interactions.

11.8. Overcoming Obstacles with Stoic Resilience

Stoicism teaches resilience and an attitude of seeing obstacles as opportunities. By confronting difficulties head-on, we strengthen our character and enhance our coping mechanisms. We learn to embrace adversity as a challenge from which we can grow and develop.

11.9. Consistent Practice for Lifelong Journey

Stoicism is not a quick fix for life's problems but a lifelong learning process. It requires consistent practice, regular self-reflection, and steadfast commitment to personal growth. By continually striving to improve ourselves, we unlock the full potential of our lives.

In conclusion, adopting Stoic philosophy in the 21st century helps us improve our lives on an individual level, subsequently radiating these benefits outward to society. Stoicism is an empowering, enriching journey that equips us to live virtuously in the modern world. It aids us in nurturing our mental fortitude, emotional resilience, and moral character. By following its guidance, we can find lasting peace and genuine contentment, regardless of life's ups and downs. Let us delve into Stoicism, embrace its virtues, and see the transformation it manifests in our lives and in the world around us.